Ice Cream

Victoria Blakemore

© 2019 Victoria Blakemore

All rights reserved. This book or parts thereof may not be reproduced in any form, stored in any retrieval system, or transmitted in any form by any means—electronic, mechanical, photocopy, recording, or otherwise—without prior written permission of the publisher, except as provided by United States of America copyright law. For permission requests, write to the publisher, at "Attention: Permissions Coordinator," at the address below.

vblakemore.author@gmail.com

Copyright info/picture credits

Cover, baibaz/Shutterstock; Page 3, Viktor/AdobeStock; Page 5, Oleg/AdobeStock; Page 7, ponce_photography/Pixabay; Page 9, Everett Collection/Shutterstock; Page 11, Yashkin Ilya/Shutterstock; Page 13, joe1719/Shutterstock; Page 15, Cathleen/AdobeStock; Page 17, Brent Hofacker/AdobeStock; Page 19, Brent Hofacker/AdobeStock; Page 21, ricka_kinamoto/AdobeStock; Page 23; very_ulissa/AdobeStock; Page 25, Moments by DeWi/AdobeStock; Page 27, olgamazina/AdobeStock; Page 29, Viktor/AdobeStock; Page 31, primipil/AdobeStock; Page 33, baibaz/Shutterstock; Page 35, pamela_d_mcadams/AdobeStock

Table of Contents

What is Ice Cream?   2

Ingredients   4

History   6

Production   10

Ice Cream Sundaes   14

Ice Cream Floats   16

Banana Splits   18

Ice Cream Sandwiches   20

Frozen Yogurt   22

Gelato   24

Sorbet   26

Sherbet   28

Ice Cream Festivals   30

Nutrition   32

Ice Cream in a Bag   34

Glossary   36

What is Ice Cream?

Ice cream is a sweet, frozen dessert. It used to be a **delicacy** that was too expensive for most people to have.

Now, ice cream is a very common treat. It is thought that 90% of American households eat ice cream.

Ice cream can be made in many different flavors. The most popular flavors of ice cream are chocolate and vanilla.

Ingredients

Ice cream is usually made using cream, milk, sugar, gelatin, and egg yolks. The dairy products used in ice cream help to give it the creamy texture.

The gelatin keeps the ice cream from forming large crystals as it freezes. The egg yolk allows the ice cream to be whipped easily.

In some restaurants chefs make ice cream to serve. It is often made using **liquid nitrogen** to help it freeze quickly.

History

There are several ideas about where ice cream came from. The first official record of ice cream was in the 1600's in Naples, Italy.

Before that time, people had been enjoying iced drinks and flavored ice, but not ice cream as we know it.

Settlers may have brought the recipes for ice cream with them to America in the 1700's.

The first ice cream factory opened in 1851 in Baltimore, Maryland. It was opened by a man named Jacob Fussell.

He sold dairy products, but had lots of extra cream. He used the cream in his ice cream factory. The ice cream was sold to restaurants and **soda fountains**.

In the 1930's, grocery stores began to sell ice cream. Before it was available in stores, ice cream was mainly sold in places like **soda fountains**.

Production

Ice cream that is sold in stores is made in large manufacturing plants. They are able to make large **quantities** of ice cream at a time.

Once they have made the ice cream it can be put into cartons. The cartons are sent to stores to sell.

First, the milk, eggs, sugar, and other ingredients are mixed in large blenders.

Next, the mixture is sent to a pasteurization machine, which heats the mixture to kill any bacteria. This is known as **pasteurizing**.

Then, the mixture is blended and allowed to rest for about eight hours. After that, flavors are added to the mixture.

Last, the mixture is frozen in large freezers. They pump air into the ice cream to make it soft and fluffy.

Ice Cream Sundaes

Ice cream sundaes are made with ice cream and toppings. Popular sauces for ice cream sundaes include hot fudge, caramel sauce, and strawberry sauce.

Chopped nuts, chocolate chips, sprinkles, and other toppings can also be added.

Ice Cream Floats

The first ice cream float was made in 1893. It was made using vanilla ice cream and root beer.

Most ice cream floats are made with vanilla ice cream. A treat called a green giant is made with lime sherbet and a lemon lime soda.

Root beer, orange soda, coke, and ginger ale are popular drinks to add to the ice cream.

Banana Splits

The banana split was first made in 1904. While they can be made many ways, most start with a banana sliced down the middle.

Scoops of chocolate, vanilla, and strawberry ice cream are put between the banana slices. They are topped with sauces, whipped cream, and a cherry.

Banana splits are often topped with chopped nuts as well. Sprinkles can be used instead.

Ice Cream Sandwiches

Ice cream sandwiches may have been first made in the 1920's. They are usually made with chocolate wafers or cookies.

Ice cream is spread between the two wafers or cookies. The sandwich is sometimes dipped in a topping like chocolate sauce, sprinkles, or chopped nuts.

Ice cream sandwiches can be made with any flavor of ice cream.

Frozen Yogurt

Frozen yogurt is very similar to ice cream, but it is made with milk instead of cream. This difference makes frozen yogurt lower in fat.

Frozen yogurt is often made with a powdered yogurt mix. It does not contain the same helpful bacteria as plain yogurt.

Frozen yogurt is often served from soft-serve machines. It comes out in a soft swirl.

Gelato

Gelato is made with milk and cream, like ice cream. However, it is made with more milk. Unlike ice cream, gelato is usually made without eggs.

Gelato is churned more slowly than ice cream. This makes it thicker because less air is whipped into it.

Gelato is stored at a warmer temperature than ice cream. This makes it softer and silkier than ice cream.

25

Sorbet

Sorbet is another kind of frozen treat. It is made with fruit and sugar. Unlike ice cream, sorbet is made without any dairy products.

Many fruits can be used to make sorbet. Pears, mangoes, strawberries, and bananas are often used to make sorbet.

Sorbet is very refreshing. It is sometimes served as a **palette cleanser** in restaurants.

Sherbet

Sherbet is very similar to sorbet. Both are made with fruit and sugar. However, sherbet is also made with milk, cream, or eggs.

The dairy that is added to the fruit and sugar make sherbet creamier than sorbet. It is lighter and has less fat than ice cream because is uses less dairy.

Sherbet can be made with fruit juice or **pureed** fruit. It is often made with oranges, limes, raspberries or lemons.

Ice Cream Festivals

Ice cream festivals are held all over the world. People come to try out new flavors and ice cream treats.

One way ice cream is made at festivals and some shops is by using a freezing cold steel plate. The cream is poured on and scraped into rolls as it freezes.

Ice cream rolls are popular at festivals because people can watch them being made.

Nutrition

Ice cream is usually high in calories, sugar, and fat. Some brands of ice cream use less sugar than others.

While ice cream may not be the healthiest of treats, it does have some health benefits. Ice cream is high in calcium. Our bones need calcium to be strong.

Ice cream also contains vitamin A and potassium. These can help you to have a healthy heart, eyes, and **immune system**.

Ice Cream in a Bag

Ingredients:

1/2 cup half and half   1 Tbs. sugar

3 cups crushed ice

1/3 cup rock salt

1/4 tsp. vanilla extract

Directions:

1. Combine half and half, vanilla, and sugar in small plastic bag.

2. Add ice and rock salt to large plastic bag.

3. Place small plastic bag inside large bag. Shake for about ten minutes.

4. Serve once ice cream is thickened.

5. Optional– add toppings such as chocolate sauce, nuts, or sprinkles

Glossary

Delicacy: something rare, uncommon

Immune System: the system in your body that helps to keep you from getting sick

Liquid Nitrogen: a liquid form of the element nitrogen, which is very cold and used to freeze things

Palate Cleanser: a food or drink that helps to clear the taste of food from the tongue so that new food is better tasted

Pasteurizing: food that is heated for a certain length of time to get rid of bacteria

Pureed: food that has been crushed or made into liquid

Quantities: amounts or numbers

Soda Fountain: a machine that pours soda. In the early to mid-1900's, soda fountains were places that sold sodas and ice cream

About the Author

Victoria Blakemore is a first grade teacher in Southwest Florida with a passion for reading.

You can visit her at

www.elementaryexplorers.com

Also in This Series

Aardvarks	Mako Sharks	Alligators	Frogs	Hedgehogs	Brown Bears	Bongos	
Sea Turtles	Quokkas	Muskrats	Zebras	Red Foxes	Ring-Tailed Lemurs	Platypuses	
Anteaters	Kangaroos	Rhinos	Jaguars	Wombats	Capybaras	Gorillas	
Cats	Skunks	Butterflies	Dingoes	Snow Leopards	African Wild Dogs	Penguins	
Whale Sharks	Wolverines	Warthogs	Caracals	Badgers	Seals	Hummingbirds	
Pikas	Humpback Whales	Pumas	Lemonade	Llamas	Tulips	Ostriches	
Sunflowers	Fennec Foxes	Sea Lions	Squirrels	Roses	Porcupines	Ice Cream	

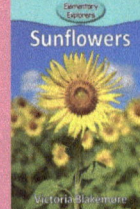

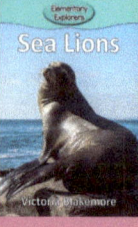

www.ingramcontent.com/pod-product-compliance
Lightning Source LLC
Chambersburg PA
CBHW041321110526
44591CB00021B/2864